Johannes C. Sikkel:

A Pioneer in Social Reform

Johannes C. Sikkel:
A Pioneer in Social Reform

by

R.H. Bremmer

Christian answers for Labour Unions, Capital and Labour, The Place of Women in Society, etc.

INHERITANCE PUBLICATIONS
NEERLANDIA, ALBERTA, CANADA
PELLA, IOWA, U.S.A.

Canadian Cataloguing in Publication Data
Bremmer, R. H.
  Johannes C. Sikkel

  Translation of: Ds. J.C. Sikkel als sociaal profeet en pionier.
  ISBN 0-921100-89-2

  1. Sikkel, Joannes Cornelis, 1856-1920. 2. Social
reformers--Netherlands--Biography. 3. Labor movement--Religious
aspects--Christianity. I. Title.
HN513.S56B7313 1998   303.48'4'092   C98-910868-6

Library of Congress Cataloging-in-Publication Data
Bremmer, R. H.
  [Ds. J.C. Sikkel als sociall profeet en pionier. English]
  Johannes c. Sikkel : a pioneer in social reform / by R.H. Bremmer.
    p. cm.
  "Christian answers for labour unions, capital and labour, the place
of women in society, etc."
  ISBN 0-921100-89-2 (pbk.)
  1. Sikkel, J. C. (Johannes Cornelis), 1856-1920. 2. Social reformers—
Netherlands—Biography. 3. Theologians—Netherlands—Biography.
4. Sociology, Christian—Netherlands. I. Title.
HN513.S56B7313 1998
303.48'4'092—dc21   98-42626
                                                                CIP

Originally published as *Ds. J.C. Sikkel als sociaal profeet en pionier*
by Uitgeverij De Vuurbaak, Barneveld, The Netherlands.
Published with permission.

Translated by Rene Vermeulen for the Free Reformed Industrial Relation
Association (Australia)

Cover design: Roelof A. Janssen

First published in English by Inheritance Publications
Box 154, Neerlandia, Alberta Canada T0G 1R0
Tel. & Fax (403) 674 3949
Web site: http://www.telusplanet.net/public/inhpubl/webip/ip.htm
E-Mail inhpubl@telusplanet.net

Published simultaneously in U.S.A. by Inheritance Publications
Box 366, Pella, Iowa 50219

Available in Australia from Inheritance Publications
Box 1122, Kelmscott, W.A. 6111 Tel. & Fax (09) 390 4940

ISBN 0-921100-89-2
                                              Printed in Canada

Contents

BIBLIOGRAPHY

Bakounin, M. *L'Empire knouto-Germanique et la révolution sociale* (1871).

Christelijke Encyclopedie, 2nd. ed.

De Ruiter, T. *Ds. J. C. Sikkel en de organisatie van de arbeid* (1950).

Fernhout, K. "In Memoriam." *Jaarboek ten dienste van de Gereformeerde Kerken in Nederland* (1921).

Gispen, W. H., Jr. *Christelijke vakorganisatie van het vak naar christelijke beginselen, Open Brief aan den Weleerw. Heer Ds. J. C. Sikkel* (1903).

Groen, P. *Gemeenschap in de arbeid.*

Hagoort, R. "Het beginsel behouden." In *Gedenkboek van het Nederlandsch Werkliedenverbond Patrimonium over de jaren 1891-1927* (1934).

Proces-verbaal der Christelijke sociale conferentie, gehouden te Amsterdam Gebouw Nieuwe Heerengracht (Patrimonium) op Maandag 9 en Dinsdag 10 Januari 1905.

Proces-verbaal van het sociaal congres gehouden te Amsterdam den 9, 10, 11, 12 November 1891 (1892).

Proces-verbaal van het Tweede christelijk sociaal congres gehouden te Amsterdam van 10 tot 13 maart 1919 (1919).

Sikkel, D. "Voorwoord." In J. C. Sikkel. *Preken*. Vol. 3 (1921).

Sikkel, J. C. *De groote toekomst en de vrouw. Een nagelaten lezing* (1920).

—. *Het loon der werklieden* (1905).

—. *Het sociale vraagstuk, bij het licht van Gods Woord* (1926).

—. *Socialisatie* (1920).

—. *Vakorganisatie naar Christelijke beginselen en vrijmaking van den arbeid* (1928).

—. *Vrijmaking van den arbeid.*

Veenhof, C. "Wat hen dreef." In *Sonnevanck 1908-1958.*

INTRODUCTION

Already from its beginning, the Calvinistic revival in the Netherlands during the nineteenth century had a strong socio-economic character. This was due, in no small measure, to its leader, Dr. Abraham Kuyper. At the outset of his public involvement, he showed that he understood the seriousness of the socio-economic question of his time. He made it clear that the gospel had consequences for societal life as well, and he soon had supporters in this view. On July 16, 1876, Klaas Kater — a bricklayer employed at *De Gekroonde Valk*, a brewery in Amsterdam owned by Willem Hovy — together with Poesiat the carpenter and some others, set up the Dutch Workers' Union, *Patrimonium*. Take note of the date: 1876 — ten years before the *Doleantie*.[1]

In the Union's constitution, the organizers asserted that their basis was the conviction "that God's Word and the traditions of our nation are the trustworthy foundations of a Christian society." Kater and Willem Hovy, his employer, felt themselves closely allied with Kuyper and his struggle. Even though one would not expect brewers to be in the forefront of Calvinist action, Willem Hovy was an exception.

The Union met with wide response both among employers and employees, and it grew steadily. In 1886, Klaas Kater was even appointed salaried director of the organization. In the meantime, the socio-economic struggle in the Netherlands had flared up on several fronts and the Christian workers, united in *Patrimonium*, became conscious of their calling and responsibility. Without doubt

---

[1] *Doleantie* means "being in mourning" — in this case, mourning over the condition of the state church. Throughout this booklet I will use the term *Doleantie* rather than Second Secession, which it is also sometimes called.

the *Doleantie* contributed to this consciousness, and so the workers began to demand a place in the Calvinistic revival which was reaching its high point at the end of the nineteenth century.

Not everyone in the circles of the *Anti Revolutionaire Partij*[2] and in other organizations was pleased with this development. This displeasure came to the fore especially when members of *Patrimonium* began to demand a place in various representative organizations. An article appeared in *De Standaard*[3] with the revealing title, "Day labourers in Parliament?" in which the author's answer to this question was clear. As a result, friction developed between *Patrimonium* and the ARP. That was the last thing Kuyper needed in those very important and crucial years. The great leader thus attended the annual general meeting of *Patrimonium* on November 10, 1890, to see what could be done to eliminate the friction. The meeting decided to ask the Central Committee of the ARP to call for a Christian Socio-Economic Congress.

On December 13, 1890, this Central Committee granted the request and thus the groundwork was laid for the First Christian Socio-Economic Congress, which was of inestimable value for the social viewpoint of the Calvinistic revival in the Netherlands. Kuyper warned the people at the outset not to be too optimistic about the outcome. He was a strategist of the first order. On December 17, 1890, he wrote in the *De Standaard* that, "providing one does not think that such a Congress will find the stone of wisdom or that in four days the most difficult problem of the day can be solved," one could expect the coming event to bear much fruit.

The Congress was thoroughly prepared: surveys were sent to all chapters of *Patrimonium* to supply the speakers with subjects for their speeches. The questions asked in the surveys were

---

[2] The *Anti Revolutionaire Partij* was Kuyper's Christian party. I will refer to it as the ARP.

[3] *De Standaard* was the leading Christian paper in the Netherlands at that time.

important and were geared to the situation of that time. The leadership of *Patrimonium* looked in every direction. Some questions were: Is church life resulting in noticeable improvements in the well-being of families among the members of *Patrimonium*? Does the preaching of the Word pay enough attention to the needs of the working classes? There were also questions such as: Do you see any advantage in providing common land in each municipality? Does it appear to be necessary for the state to provide welfare for sick or elderly workers? Is it desirable to have an additional day off each week besides Sunday or to introduce some additional holidays apart from the feast days?

On November 9, 1891, the Congress, which had taken longer to organize than anticipated, met in Amsterdam. The patron of the Congress was Mr. Aeneas Baron Mackay. Dr. Kuyper became chairman, and A. F. de Savornin Lohman deputy chairman. There were more than five hundred participants from all classes of society, as well as — and this must also be mentioned — from various church-groups. The severity of the struggle of the *Doleantie* had not yet forced such a separation that confessing Christians were unable to meet at this congress to discuss one of the most difficult problems of that time.

Kuyper (who else?) delivered the opening speech. It was grandiose in design and is still worth reading. He started by quoting some familiar lines from the Dutch poet, Willem Bilderdijk: "When a nation must perish in its sins, the 'leprosy of the soul' *in the church* begins." Kuyper then reminded his audience about Groen van Prinsterer,[4] who, already in 1853, had spoken of the truth contained in socialism "which gives it strength," and who reminded his supporters that "socialism finds its origin in the revolution"

---

[4] Mr. Guillaume Groen van Prinsterer, 1801-1876, a Christian historian, publicist, statesman, and political leader. While serving the Dutch King at Brussels, he came under the preaching of Merle d'Aubigne, the court preacher, and thus came to a warm commitment to the Reformed faith.

and, as revolution, can "be conquered only by Christianity." According to Kuyper, it cannot be denied that there is a direct link between the socio-economic question and the Christian faith.

He pointed out that the origin of the social question was to be found (a) in the French Revolution, which had torn up the old order in society, and (b) in modern industrialization, which caused the law of the animal world — that the trout swallows the fly — to become the law of all socio-economic relations.

Kuyper concluded from this that the socio-economic question was not a matter of philanthropy but of an architectonic critique of society. He warned against underestimating the seriousness of the issue. It would be safe to say, according to Kuyper, "that the socio-economic question had become *the* question, the burning question at the end of the nineteenth century." Many in the Netherlands are suffering, he went on, "not so much among the regular tradesmen but among the proletariat behind them." To support his argument, he reminded his audience of the recent troubles in the province of Friesland.

As far as the positive part of his speech is concerned, we point to his emphasis on the Christian's stewardship. He taught his audience "that all we own is only *on loan*, all our assets are part of our stewardship." This instruction has since borne much fruit in Christian social organizations. Kuyper pleaded for a labour law as well as one for commerce, pointing out that the state has a task in this connection, even though it must still respect the sovereignty of each sphere. Kuyper ended with the prayer, "that it would never be said of the Dutch Christians that, through our own fault, through the lukewarmness of the Christian faith of both the upper and lower classes, the salvation of our society was hindered and the blessing of God the Father forfeited."

The congress had been well planned. The participants were split into three groups. The first and most important group dealt with the socio-economic question and the Christian religion. The preparatory committee had appointed the following speakers for this group: Dr. H. Bavinck, Dr. F. van Gheel Gildemeester (a popular *Hervormd* [Dutch "state" church] minister from The Hague), Rev. A. Brummelkamp Jr., Prof. Dr. W. Geesink, and, the youngest of the five, Rev. J. C. Sikkel (minister of the *Nederduits* [or *Doleantie*] Reformed Church in The Hague). Rev. Sikkel introduced this subject: "What principles does Holy Scripture present for the family and its individual members with regard to labour?"

It was the first time that Rev. Johannes Cornelis Sikkel appeared in the national spotlight. He was now 35 years old and had been a minister for only six years. That he had been included in this group with such well-known men as Bavinck and Geesink indicates that his interest in social questions was already known in wider circles at that time. Sikkel had been ordained as a minister on February 25, 1883, in the *Hervormd* congregation of Biezelinge (in the province of Zeeland). In 1885, he went to Hijlaard in Friesland. There he became involved in the *Doleantie* movement which would shake *Hervormd* Friesland on its foundations. On January 17, 1886, Sikkel and his congregation joined the *Doleantie*, and he soon became one of the provincial leaders of the movement. On November 18, 1888, he became minister of the *Doleantie* church at The Hague. It is known that he attempted to pay a family visit to King Willem III because for a time he still considered all members of the *Hervormd* congregation to be members of the *Doleantie* church.

Sikkel was the son of Arnold Sikkel, health inspector at Utrecht, and Annetta Carolina van Ellekom. He was born on November 18, 1856. Because of the Belgian revolt, his father had gotten into financial difficulties, and Sikkel learned in his youth what it meant to be poor. He received his primary education under the well-known teacher Van Lummel and followed in his mentor's career. His first position was in the Christian school at Voorschoten, his second in Zeist. It was there that Rev. Nahuys noticed the gifts this fiery teacher had and he helped him to take up the study of

theology. In 1878, he passed the entrance exam at the University
of Utrecht and enrolled as a student. During his years of study he
had to find ways and means to fend for himself. Because of that
he was unable to participate in student activities, a fact that
coloured his personality from that point on.

In 1883, Kuyper published his pamphlet, *Treatise on the
Reformation of the Churches*. It made such an impression on Sikkel
that from then on he was an ardent and faithful follower of the
leader of the Calvinistic revival. He remained such until his death.
According to Sikkel's biographer, Dr. T. de Ruiter, Sikkel had
great influence in The Hague "because of his imposing personality,
his prophetical tone, and fascinating viewpoints." Both
theologically and socially, he stood out from the majority of
Kuyper's disciples in the early decades of the twentieth century.

This is not the place for us to discuss Sikkel as a theologian
and a preacher. That is a separate subject. It is impossible, however,
to see him as a socio-economic prophet apart from the theological
viewpoints which became evident in his preaching throughout the
years. Sikkel was an original man. In a very short time he developed
his own theological viewpoint. While it is true that he had acquired
his initial impulse and main ideas from Kuyper, he gave them a
form which was entirely his own. We would characterize this form
as a Christ-centred world and life view. All that Sikkel wrote —
his large and still valuable commentary on the Book of Genesis,
entitled *The Book of Births* (1906), his various Bible studies, his
meditations, his sermons — are permeated with this Christ-centred
viewpoint.

Sikkel was not a learned theologian in the usual sense of the
term. He was never completely able to overcome the disadvantage
of not having studied Greek and Hebrew. Someone who expected
a philological exposition of Scripture, based on the original
languages, would be disappointed, but that disadvantage was well
compensated in his Scripture studies and sermons by his prophetical
viewpoint on life and the world. J. C. Rullman, who knew him

personally, writes, "Every sermon reflected his whole world view in miniature." He knew and expounded what it means "to live by the light of Scripture, through Christ as the light of the world." Rullman also wrote that Sikkel was able "to show clearly the main points of the struggle of that time."

In 1899, Sikkel accepted a call to Amsterdam. He would labour there until 1920, the year of his death. In Amsterdam he stopped writing his sermons in full, Rev. Fernhout tells us in his obituary; his sermons were given birth on the pulpit after thorough study at home. Many of his sermons were recorded by stenographers and were published after his death by his followers for the benefit of the Sikkel Fund. Even today they are fresh and useful for anyone who does not want to stop at the explanation of the text but want to apply God's Word to the issues of the day.

Sikkel the theologian and preacher was the same person as Sikkel the socio-economic prophet. In this latter role, however, he made an important contribution to the Christian socio-economic movement, and we will examine this contribution in this study. By looking at his life's work, struggles, and writings in chronological order we will gain a better understanding of him than by a systematic analysis of his thinking. For that, we direct interested readers to the study by the (Roman Catholic) Dr. de Ruiter which was published in 1950. Even though De Ruiter, as is to be expected, has some difficulty following a Reformed man like Sikkel in certain details, it must be said that his study gives a valuable overview of Sikkel's thinking along with a thoughtful evaluation.

I

Sikkel as a speaker at the First Christian Socio-Economic Congress (1891)

At the First Christian Socio-Economic Congress, Sikkel had been asked to introduce the subject of what principles Holy Scripture presents "for the family and its individual members with regard to labour." In this speech, we already recognize the later Sikkel. Even though his thinking on various points changed, his basic ideas remained the same. This first speech also displays the same colour and prophetical ardour that would make his later writings so captivating.

He began by presenting what Scripture says about labour, and with that we immediately encounter one of his basic ideas. Although he might later take a somewhat different approach to the practical outworking of his ideas, his basic ideas remained the same. He refused to limit human labour to manual labour alone. No, labour "belongs to the life of man as God's image bearer." God uses man, with his labour, to tend and keep the garden "to complete the work of God." The curse, which was placed on labour through man's fall, brought with it increased difficulty in that labour. The earth must now be *forced* to produce its fruit.

But through the covenant of grace, labour is saved; it is now bound to the covenant of grace. Christ saves labour — and with that statement we are at the heart of Sikkel's Christ-centred view of life. "When He rose from the dead, Christ also reconciled labour, saved it, and raised it from the dead." After Pentecost, the gospel calls labour "out of prison" and restores it "as a means of serving and glorifying the Lord." The gospel not only comforts the worker, but it also delivers him from the "bondage of slavery." The work of man has a dual purpose: it is man's service to God with regard to the world and humanity and, at the same time, it is a means to provide man with a livelihood. That latter task has now been given to the head of the family. In this way, Sikkel moved from his fundamental view of labour to his real topic: the Scriptural view of the family based on the divine calling in labour.

In the practical outworking of this subject it is noteworthy that Sikkel had his eye on the *man*, first of all. For the *woman* he hardly saw a task in this field. Later he would come to think differently about that! The woman's only task is in the family. But even in saying this Sikkel was not entirely consistent since he did want to allow the woman to participate in "light field work" and in helping with the animals, but he considered work away from home impermissible. Work in the field, in the workshop, or in the factory he considered to be in conflict "with the rule laid down by God." Working in the home was different, since Scripture mentioned spinning, sewing, womanly handiwork, cooking, and baking in the well-known passage in Proverbs 31. Should the woman become a widow and have to act as head of the family, then, for example, minor retail trade would be allowed. As if what he saw as the rule of Scripture — if it was indeed a rule of Scripture — no longer applied then!

Still, there were also progressive elements in this speech in 1891. Sikkel insisted that the father who controlled his children's income should do so in consultation with them. Here we already find the idea of consultation which was a characteristic of Sikkel's approach and which we find in many of his later writings. As far as that is concerned there is nothing new under the sun.

Already at this time he made a powerful plea for a just wage, an idea he would later develop in detail. "The *employer* should offer sufficient wages so that the *husband* would be able to support his family without the need for his wife to earn wages." The wages should be such that the husband has time to spend with his family. This was an important idea when long working hours were the common rule. Furthermore, the employer should encourage the employee to acquire his own property; "owning one's *own* house enhances home life, the worker's person, and his work." And what is especially important, Sikkel stressed that, in the case of an employee's accident or death, the employer should recognize his duty toward the worker and his family by making timely provisions for such events.

Moreover, the government should ensure that it did not do injustice to the workers in the Netherlands or, Sikkel added significantly, in the colonies. International consultation is essential in these questions. Here we see for the first time something that reappears time and again in Sikkel's writings, namely that his view went beyond the borders of the Netherlands. He fought throughout his whole life for an international orientation of the Christian workers' movement and politics.

During the discussion, people asked questions of both a principial and a practical nature. Dr. Geesink sprang to the defense of women telegraphists and asked if girls were required to be "kitchen princesses" forever. In his answer, Sikkel explained that to him it was a thorn in his flesh when he saw a woman working at the post office or the telegraph office. "Our women are too good for that," Sikkel said. (The report of the congress noted applause here.) According to him, girls did have a task at kindergartens because the emphasis there was on nurture rather than on teaching. He was opposed to higher educational institutions for girls, because this would be an absurdity. According to the report of the congress, this statement was heartily approved by the brothers.

Questions about principles came up as well. Dr. H. Bavinck could not accept Sikkel's Christ-centred world view. He wanted to know if labour did not have its own place in the creation order apart from the covenant of grace. Sikkel's answer was that creation was saved "only through the grace of Christ Jesus." To Gheel

Gildemeester, who made a similar remark, he explained that in Christ all things are reconciled. This view contained, in seed form, a criticism of Kuyper's teaching on common grace, a criticism which S. G. de Graaf, on whom Sikkel's "prophet's mantle" fell, later developed into a thorough critique of Kuyper's teaching on common grace from the standpoint of Christ as Saviour. Sikkel himself often speaks of common grace, but never in a way which obscures the view of Christ's resurrection as the redemption of the world.

II

Sikkel's forty theses (1903)

When Sikkel moved to Amsterdam in 1899, he found a congregation under the leadership of Rev. B. van Schelven, one of the great patrician figures from the circle of *Doleantie* ministers. Van Schelven had been married twice to aristocratic ladies, and here came Sikkel, a full-fledged democrat. No wonder he sometimes had difficulties in Amsterdam. We see something of his clash with the powers there in his writings from that time in the *Church Bulletin of Holland*. In 1905, this bulletin became his own paper — renamed *Hollandia* — in which he expounded his ideas until 1916.

Take note of the fierceness with which he expresses himself in 1902: "Stop locking up the Gospel in your church." Christianity is not characterized by philanthropy. Those times are gone. "No sermons for the poor or schools for the poor, no pews for the poor or homes for the poor, and no food for the poor or goods for the poor — this approach is not in accord with the Gospel." We must certainly struggle against the socialists, but at the same time, "as much as possible, we must make human society conform to the Gospel." And with regard to the growing workers' association, those who stand by watching "represent the time of their grandfathers." Earlier he had written: "We are not finished when we say to each other, socialists are evil men. Take off your blinkers."

Indeed, Sikkel would not stand by watching — not that he was given a lot of opportunity for that. During the turbulent year of 1903 he suddenly found himself in the midst of the struggle and, perhaps to his own surprise, he found himself in sharp conflict with the Christian socio-economic movement. Sikkel, who, more than anyone else, had taken up the cause of the working man! It must have caused him a lot of heartache.

In February 1903 — Kuyper had become Prime Minister in 1901 — a railway strike broke out unexpectedly. Both the government and the public were surprised. There were abuses and injustices in the national railway system, but no one expected the explosion when it came. The government took measures: anti-strike bills were submitted to the Second Chamber of the Dutch Parliament and the Army was brought in. The atmosphere in the country was tense. In reaction to Kuyper's anti-strike laws, the socialist workers' movement called for a general strike in April 1903: "All the wheels stop, if your mighty arm demands it!" The Roman Catholic and Protestant Christian workers did not participate; they supported the government. The general strike collapsed like a leaking balloon.

In the meantime, these months foreboded a severe confrontation with the power of the modern workers' movement. This also influenced Christian circles in which the trade union movement was in its infancy. *Patrimonium* and the later Christian trade union movement had a mother and daughter relationship to each other. Certain groups of workers from within *Patrimonium* had begun to form separate trade unions. In 1900, the so-called Christian labour secretariat was established under the auspices of *Patrimonium*. At about the same time, the leadership of *Patrimonium* passed from Klaas Kater to Rev. A. S. Talma, who also became a member of the Second Chamber for the ARP in 1901.

On June 2, 1903, a brochure entitled *Where Do We Go With Trade Unionism?* and signed with the pseudonyms Q. and N. served as a discussion item at a meeting of the board of *Patrimonium*. Talma was violently opposed to the publication of this paper because it questioned the necessity of a trade union movement. Trade unions were tolerated as expedient for the movement, the authors said, but they were not a cure. Apparently the brochure had been influenced by what had occurred that spring. Talma, who was convinced of the need for a Christian trade union movement and gave it his wholehearted support, considered it a dangerous brochure.

Shortly after, on June 17, 1903, the Christian employers' federation, "Boaz," with whom *Patrimonium* cooperated at that time, held their annual meeting. Prof. H. Bavinck gave a speech entitled, "What is the calling of the employer toward his employees?" and Rev. J. C. Sikkel followed with a speech entitled, "What is the calling of the employer toward the trade union movement?" Since Prof. Bavinck's speech went over time, Sikkel had little opportunity to explain and defend the forty theses he had previously submitted. They were, however, published in the magazine put out by "Boaz"; *Patrimonium* published them in the July 16, 1903, issue of its magazine. Talma immediately started a series of four articles attacking Sikkel's theses. The last of these articles was published on August 20, 1903.

It was clear that Sikkel had dropped a bombshell into the ranks of the Christian socio-economic movement; the commotion he had caused was not small. Why was this? Reading these theses now, one is impressed with the broad sweep of his ideas. Here we find a man expressing himself concerning the social issues — about which he had thought long and hard — in an attempt to find a solution. The problem was that, in his train of thought about the difficult questions of the day, he reached out to a future yet to be created. That proved calamitous.

What becomes apparent immediately in the forty theses is a totally new way of using the words "trade union movement." Sikkel published his theses under the title *Trade unionism according to Christian principles*. At that time, everyone associated trade unions with the growing working men's societies. These societies aimed to improve the position of working men over against employers. Sikkel, however, used the phrase "trade union organization" to speak of what is known today as an industrial organization. The different interpretations of the same phrase caused much confusion. Furthermore, Sikkel's principled choice for industrial organization meant that the workers' movement, the growing trade union organization, did not receive his support. Looking at the debates within *Patrimonium* which we mentioned earlier, it is understandable that his forty theses offended many.

Sikkel divided his theses into three groups. The first he entitled, "The current so-called trade union organization," in which he stated that he considered the current trade union movement to be a great danger. By forcing the workers to join the organization, the trade union movement was able to control the power within the workplace by means of the weapon of the strike. In his eleventh thesis, Sikkel says that the trade union movement "is nothing more than an organized class struggle."

In the second group of theses he dealt with "The calling of employers with regard to the current trade union movement." That calling, according to Sikkel, was to resist, "in God's name," the so-called trade union movement. Employers from their side should resist the temptation to organize themselves into employers' federations. By doing so, they themselves were accepting the class struggle. They should only negotiate with their own employees, if necessary, by means of worker spokesmen. Moreover, they should deliberate about the true and real organization of their trade.

That was the concern of the last group of theses, "The true industrial and trade organization." This part presented the positive aspects of his view. They were broad in scope. He wanted the enterprise — the industrial concern — to be seen as "an organic cooperative community of people." This organic community had to be organized in the true trade movement. To Sikkel, all of this came together in the so-called labour contract made applicable to each industrial concern. That was, after all, what the whole socio-economic struggle of that time was focused on: the establishment of labour contracts in the larger companies. It would have to be, according to Sikkel, "the bond which ties each worker to the enterprise."

His vision went farther than wages and working hours alone. The contract would also give guidance and rules for worker participation in the running of the industrial community. Furthermore, the worker would have to leave some of his income in the hands of the enterprise and thereby acquire the right to share in the surplus profit of the company, in proportion to their share in the firm's capital.

In his 38th thesis, he expressed his ideal in the following manner: "*Fellowship in enterprise* is the ideal of the true trade organization." In prophetical language and vision, he went on to say that the enterprise "seeks the fulfilment of a great task: the Grand Enterprise." He thought in broad and far-reaching perspectives in a time when very little of such thought had been able to mature. In thesis 39 he even expressed the desire that individual enterprises be united in an organized trade community for the support of particular firms. This trade community would be charged with the responsibility to act as arbiter and promote training in trade skills. Furthermore, he considered it desirable that these trade communities would also seek international organization.

Today, after so many years, it is clear what Sikkel's vision was all about: he was absolutely opposed to separate organizations of workers and employers. He sought organized contact between employers and their employees only in concrete individual enterprises, by means of spokesmen, in order to bring about in this way the organization of the individual trade communities, which in turn would organize that particular trade nationally and internationally. There was no place in his thinking for separate trade and employers' organizations.

When he later published his *Explanation*, Sikkel developed these theses further. As a starting point he took the French Revolution which had torn apart the long-established guilds and its pattern of close ties between workmen and employers. This led to the destruction of small business by big business and to the mastery of capital at the expense of labour. In that emergency situation, the workers used their right to federate, seeing it as a favour from God at a time of revolution. As a result he then wrote — no doubt because of the storm of criticism he had received — "Workers' clubs are not to be condemned; Christian Workers' clubs are necessary." He added, however, that such clubs are not trade organizations. Therefore, he went on, he wanted *Patrimonium* and the Christian Employers' federation to come together to plan and unite "for the regulation of the true — but not currently existing — Trade Organization." As things were at the time, the trade union movement was destroying employership by forcing employers to bow to the demands of trade unions. It is evident that he was still under the impression of the troubles of that past spring when he stated that "through God's goodness we have had a sign, a prophecy, a warning in the first months of 1903." Characteristically, Sikkel went on with these words: "The crowds gather from all sides, from all countries, with all means, to besiege organized human life, which tries to maintain resistance. . . . Anarchy only brings victory to Workers' power."

In his *Explanation*, Sikkel underscored in powerful terms that true organization could come from individual enterprise only, from the employers and those who work with them in their business — that is the only trade organization which God desires. Therefore "Boaz" and *Patrimonium* must begin to consult in concert?

In explaining the third group of theses, Sikkel again emphasized that trade is "a community of human life in independent businesses and enterprises." Labour is not a material, not a product, not a number, but it is "a part of life — human life — which bears living fruit and is connected to that fruit by common interest." Once again, we are at the heart of Sikkel's biblical vision of labour. The unhealthy situation was not the low wages or the long working hours but the lack of love which regards man as a tool of trade and a hired hand. There was no escaping this, Sikkel wrote: "our age leaves us no choice; the machine, the division of labour, the competition, the development of industry demand the great and the greatest enterprise." This great enterprise was not a cooperative but an organism. For that reason, Sikkel maintained that there should be authority in the establishment — sovereignty — but that sovereignty has rights and duties which must be firmly laid down in any labour contract as the constitution of the community of labour.

This was indeed a new idea in the circles of those who, in the first years of the twentieth century, were struggling to enhance the socio-economic viewpoint of the Calvinistic revival. They were striving to get a Christian trade union movement off the ground in opposition to the one in the Socialist camp, and now they heard from Sikkel, one of their leaders, that their movement was not what God wanted. Is it any wonder that Talma, an extremely practical person, became very annoyed?

From his side, Sikkel tried to pour oil on the troubled waters. In the September 3, 1903, issue of his magazine, *Hollands Kerkblad*, he wrote that organizations such as *Patrimonium* and its various trade organizations were necessary, but that the workers' organizations were not trade organizations. He therefore advised *Patrimonium* and "Boaz" to establish a committee to work out the way in which the organization of labour could develop into a trade organization according to Christian principles. Again this was too much for Talma. He answered that it was not proper first to praise the Christian trade organization and then to suggest establishing a committee to act as if this organization did not exist and to determine how it ought to be.

III

Polarization around the forty theses

In such an atmosphere, *Patrimonium* met in Utrecht for its annual meeting on September 7 and 8, 1903. Several groups introduced motions to condemn Sikkel's theses. The discussion was impassioned. Van der Molen, one of the group leaders, remarked about Sikkel that he "with a great sickle [*sikkel* is Dutch for "sickle"] cut off the feet of the reapers. . . ." Van der Molen proposed a censure motion which concluded that the right of the workers to unite with others and thus ensure better working conditions must be maintained. An amendment by Rev. W. H. Gispen Jr. was accepted by the meeting. It called on all Christian workers to support their trade union with all their might. The motion was passed with 78 votes for and 7 against.

Sikkel immediately defended himself in *De Standaard*, stating that when he composed his theses he had not, in any way, thought of *Patrimonium*. Rev. Gispen responded in an "open letter," however, by asking what Sikkel had been thinking of when he wrote about the "so-called Christian trade union organization" in theses 12 and 13.

Sikkel found himself in the situation of a man who suddenly discovers that his words had an entirely different effect than he had intended and now he sought by various means to douse the fires. That wasn't easy, for Rev. W. H. Gispen Jr.'s "Open Letter" appeared already in October 1903. His criticism of Sikkel was severe. Gispen was a practical man. With Kuyper in *De Standaard*, he considered that Sikkel had unrealistic dreams of the future and, according to Kuyper, this should not in any way check the progress of the courageously commenced private organization of the Christian workers.

Moreover, he severely criticized Sikkel's ideals: "I see in the idea of joint enterprise the beginning of a *socialistic* principle, which, should it receive general support, would lead to the socialist, communistic ideal." In this system, the employer becomes the first owner, but the regular employees are owners along with him. Should the business start to lose money, it would also impact the workers.

Still, Gispen was not opposed to socio-economic change through governmental action, but he thought that the law should determine the maximum profit in an enterprise; the rest should, following certain rules, benefit the workers. Furthermore, he considered Sikkel's idea that the workers be represented in the running of the business excellent. Gispen's basic view, however, remained unchanged: there will always be a struggle between the interests of capital and labour; the most idealistic work organization cannot overcome that. According to Gispen, Sikkel failed to see that. Perhaps something could be achieved should the Chambers of Labour (which were still in existence then) receive binding authority.

Thus, the development of the still young Christian social-economic movement showed a polarizing trend in 1903. Gispen's "Open Letter" had only just been published when the employers' organization, "Boaz," held its annual meeting on November 16, 1903. It wholeheartedly supported Sikkel's theses. At that annual meeting the opponents — Talma and Sikkel — were both present and entered into a debate with each other. Talma was bitter, considering that his life's work for the Christian trade union movement was being demolished. He spoke harsh words. The minutes of the meeting note that at the end of the meeting he sincerely apologized for the tone of his speech. That too was possible!

IV

Sikkel's answer to the polarization: liberation of labour

Sikkel felt that something had to happen. He went to work and, in a short time, wrote his *Liberation of Labour* as an answer to Rev. W. H. Gispen Jr. It became his most important publication in the socio-economic field. Working hard within a very short time frame, he put the whole of his heart of social concern into this publication. It is a book of 154 pages and is still worth reading. It appeared under the motto: "Jesus said to her, 'Did I not say to you that if you would believe you would see the glory of God?' " (John 11:40). Sikkel explored what he felt was the issue in his era, viewing matters from a prophetical perspective. Modern industrial development could not be halted; it would reach a height which would "open the storehouse of God's creation" — a grand vision! In that development, capital lords it over labour and enslaves the whole fellowship of labour. Only the hourly rate and its connected fringe benefits would be for the labourer. It was the weapon of the hourly wage that capital used to attack labour and the commonweal.

Gispen had accused Sikkel that his theses had been written under the influence of the events of that spring. Sikkel denied it. He had made an thorough study of what he called "the movement," the modern socialist movement. This movement emanated from Hegel's philosophical idea of the "origin" of all things, which Marx in turn had formulated and systematized as historical (materialistic) evolution. The "movement" had two forms: a political and an economic form. Its aim was to conquer the state of the capitalists. Marx was not concerned about business or trade as such but only with victory over the ruling class by the workers. Marx wanted anarchy as a transitional measure, but there were already socialists who wanted it as a permanent state. Michael Bakounin was their man, their prophet. Sikkel quotes Bakounin as saying that "the devil is the creator of freedom; we must have the devil in us." Bakounin formulated the saying that Marx is the brain and Bakounin the soul, the will of the movement. Domela Nieuwenhuis (the Dutch socialist leader): that was Bakounin!

Behind all of this lay the great socio-economic issue: the fact that the workers had no rights in their labour. Who, asked Sikkel, could have a human heart and evade this issue? He now declared emphatically that he wanted to accept the Christian trade union movement. Only it should not seek its power in breaking the "movement."

According to Sikkel, Rev. Gispen evaluated the situation much "too superficially and too lightly" and therefore his advice would be too light. He had the following sentence printed with emphasis added: "*one remains in the relationships created by liberalism.*" The workers deliberated with Rev. Gispen how to wage war, but "war excludes consultation and consultation excludes war."

Sikkel's heart mourned the social situation: "A whole host of our nation — good solid men, through whose effort our nation and our industry could flourish — are consumed by the hatred of members of the movement." And therefore we must "not demonize the socialists."

Next, Sikkel dealt with what he saw as the ideal. In this he hooked in on what Kuyper had proclaimed as the aim at the first Christian socio-economic conference: architectonic critique of human society. Many in Christian social circles had moved no further than the contents of that opening speech. But progress was needed. To that end, Sikkel developed his own vision of society. It maintained the idea of society as an organism, reflecting the ideas of Kuyper and Bavinck. Society is a "living human organism." Against Rev. Gispen, who had found him idealistic and complained about his many writings about all sorts of questions, Sikkel retorted, "Marx has defeated thousands with his organization, but with his reprehensible fundamental formula his ten thousands."

He then went on to give a thorough explanation of principles. He saw the work community as an organic living fellowship of people called by God to labour. Even in the case of the worst slavery such a work community exists. Sikkel understood the term "organizing" to mean restoring and ordering the organism of labour as created and willed by God. Organization must connect into what is available in the organism and he wholeheartedly rejected the claim that this had anything to do with the making of an artificial flower in place of a real flower, as *Patrimonium* had said when it reproached him. In every organism there is a law at work, and the government must assist the worker when this law is flouted in the working community.

Here we clearly see Sikkel giving expression to his ideas in terms of the idea of sphere sovereignty. He was a good pupil of Kuyper, who had tried to make his ideas useful for the socio-economic sphere. Sikkel was concerned with moral rights in the work community. In a long quotation, he says: "Love demands — in the name of justice, of humanity, of human fellowship, in the name of Christ, of God's Word, of the common grace of God, of the love of God for His humankind — *organization of labour in fellowship*, not arbitrarily, but according to the divine right of the organic community, *through regular determination and the maintenance of everyone's rights and duties.*" "*That*," he emphasized, "*is the liberation of Labour.*" He capitalized the word "labour." He meant to indicate in this way that he was thinking not only of the contribution made by the workers in the community, but of the whole organism of the enterprise. "What a rich treasure of life God gives to thousands, who as free men join hands in

Labour!" He continued, alluding to a well-known drawing by Albert Hahn: "That, by the grace of God, is the mighty arm which does not halt the wheel of Labour, but which makes it work in honour for the coming generation." As Sikkel saw it, in the fellowship of labour the employer is not a lump of capital, but is to be honoured as head of that fellowship.

Sikkel drafted his practical projects on the basis of this principle. The fellowship of labour must first of all be developed within private enterprise. His starting point was the labour contract out of which he developed his ideas. In this way, there came into existence what he called "a constitutional fellowship of labour," which rested on two principles: (a) the acknowledgment of the moral rights of the employees; and (b) the authoritative rights of the employer.

He did not want to stop at individual enterprises, however. They should organize themselves into a community of all the enterprises in that particular trade, respecting at all times the sphere sovereignty in the individual enterprises. This trade community should look after the interests of the trade, including training, and should determine the required levels of skill and hand out trade certificates. It should also form a trade council together with a trade arbitration court. The government in turn should legislatively acknowledge the public right in Labour, as it had organically developed.

Finally, Sikkel discussed the relationship of the government to free initiative in the area of labour. He saw the state absolutism of the Liberals as the cause of anarchism and, in this context, he even spoke — with a wonderfully broad view — of "a certain right" of anarchism. He stood up for the rights of the individual. He pointed in that context to Russia: remember this was 1903!

In considering the task of the government, Sikkel struggled with the idea of sphere sovereignty. On the one hand, this idea forbade intervention by the government in the sphere of labour; on the other hand, Sikkel realized that without government intervention nothing could be achieved. The idea of sphere sovereignty was clearly a brake on the development of his ideas.

In fact, he came to propagate a corporative state: he advocated a Chamber of Labour next to a political Chamber. In this chamber, Labour could determine its rights with state authority. These were dreams of the future, and he realized that. Therefore, in what he called the emergency situation, he sought the basis for government intervention. Immediate legislative action should be taken so that aged people could receive the bread which they earned with their labour. Consideration should be given to the extent to which the State treasury could be used to bridge the gap toward assuring the right in labour for these old people. Sikkel was well ahead of his time.

Sikkel struggled with great difficulties here, for if the government was allotted the task to regulate labour it would lead to an election struggle in which the winner would take all. He detested this thought. On the other hand, he saw that there were national interests which demanded united action, such as electricity and water. He asked, "What about the national soil?" Later, he was not averse to a form of nationalization of the soil. He finally sought the solution of this difficulty in this way: the government would need to force the realization of a just labour contract, in which he wanted to include provisions in case of accident and old age, the development of legal structures in the fellowship of labour, justice, and participation in management. It was clearly a corporative ideal. He ended this section by speaking of a public acknowledgment of organized labour within legal restraints which would apply in the life of the corporative nation and state.

In the meantime, Sikkel was still faced with a difficulty. How could he, by means of this apology, clear up his disagreement with the growing Christian trade union movement? This is how he solved it. Having arrived at the end of his discourse, he made a strong appeal for private initiative in the socio-economic sphere. To stimulate the communication between employers and employees he wanted an labour contract published, in which the rights and responsibilities of both sides would be laid down. To back his call, he pointed to the firm of Stork in Hengelo. That firm's labour contract included the provision of profit sharing, insurance against sickness and accident, and pensions for widows and orphans. They also had a representative body, "*de Kern*" (the Kernel).

Referring to the Christian trade union movement, he wrote, "Every suggestion that I do not appreciate these unions is based on a misrepresentation." He viewed the union's task as taking the initiative in the proposals put forward by him. "They must raise the banner for the liberation of Labour. They must win the sympathy of both Workers and Employers. They can open the way which leads to a solution." For this to happen, it was necessary that Christian workers would unite in trade unions.

In this context Sikkel pleaded for an international court of arbitration; he had a wide-ranging view. The early years of the twentieth century were anarchistic, he concluded, and yet "the saving love of Christ is joyously proclaimed over the whole world."

V

Sikkel and Talma at the Christian Socio-Economic Conference of 1905: the end of polarization

Naturally, Sikkel's *Liberation* did not solve the disagreements. The parties remained sharply divided; the progress of the social movement within the Calvinistic revival seemed blocked. During the course of 1904, that became apparent to both "Boaz" (employers) and *Patrimonium* (employees), and they consulted each other about it. There is something touching in the fact that despite all the troubles of those years the parties did not abandon but sought each other.

In the end, they agreed to convene a Christian Socio-Economic Conference. Mr. D. J. de Geer (who later became a minister) took the chairman's gavel. The conference was held in the headquarters of *Patrimonium* in Amsterdam. The attendance was good: three hundred participants from throughout the country. The topic for discussion that day was the general task of the trade unions. The speakers were Rev. A. S. Talma and Rev. J. C. Sikkel. The aim was to reach agreement.

The two streams within the Christian social movement clearly came to the fore in the two speeches. Talma was a warm supporter of the trade unions. He regarded them as a safeguard against exploitation of labour by capital. Their aim was to achieve a reasonable labour contract. "We need to plough the social soil to sow seed which will bear fruit till the next century." By organizing in unions the workers received responsibility. "I believe," declared Talma, "that nothing greater can be imagined than when people learn to accept responsibility." In that, both speakers were of one mind.

Sikkel's speech dug deeper. He maintained his ideals as he had enunciated them in 1903 but at the same time tried to get as close to the other party as possible. He saw a double emergency in society: (a) the total lack of a reasonable labour law; and (b) the influence of the unchristian spirit in the unions. He therefore pleaded again for the establishment of a responsible trade constitution by means of a collective labour contract. The organizations of Christian employers and employees could support such a contract and the formulation of it; its *acceptance*, according to him, remained the business of employers and employees within the individual enterprises. He desired an initial "collective opinion" of these groups, which would, however, become law when the employers and employees themselves had approved it *personally*. The same should apply, according to Sikkel, in the case of proposed strike action, which ought to be evaluated *personally*. To him, strikes and support for agreements remained a personal, moral decision.

Again, he hammered home his theme that the labour contract should not only deal with hourly rates of pay and the number of working hours, but should also include provisions for sickness, accident, old age, and death. Furthermore, when the agreements had been established there would be a place for Christian trade unions to educate and stimulate.

He emphasized once again that his first concern was not the question of wages and the distribution of wealth, but the moral relationships between people. "By people's working together, a fellowship of labour is established." The rule for that fellowship is "love your neighbour as yourself," and "consider the other more excellent than yourself." This rule applied to both small as well as big business.

Sikkel sought the establishment of a different society, one in which both capital and labour were done justice to by means of written laws. In a certain way this would make trade unions superfluous, but they would retain their use as training institutions.

The debate generated a lot of heat. Some spoke of Sikkel's ideas as "old hat" and were called to order by the chairman. Talma thought Sikkel's approach would make the unions powerless because all they could do would be to advise. Sikkel reacted with zest against the "old hat" accusation: "the speaker had not disposed of any of his hats." Even Sikkel felt the need to camouflage his change of course.

He then said some important things. In the first place, the Christian trade unions needed to know very well what they wanted. He added that for him the trade unions "were dear to his heart." He described their task as follows: to maintain society as it is, but also to reform it according to Christian moral principles." The aim was to win hearts and consciences. "God sometimes uses half a century, sometimes only a few years for a movement to have effect" — words which have lost none of their relevance.

And Sikkel again hammered home his theme: no matter how poor the circumstances, there is a community of labour, and within it the struggle for rights and responsibilities must be waged. Consultation must take place within the enterprise, no matter how difficult the situation: "Anyone who is walking along the right path is always certain of that guiding hand which smoothes the way, opens the door." In that way, a written labour law should come about.

Even though there were other items of business at this conference, the debate between the two social grandmasters were the most important. At the end of the conference, a resolution was adopted which betrayed the hand and point of view of Talma, but in which Sikkel's vision was also given a place.

Talma: "The aim of the trade union is to help the workers in their endeavour for a better legal position within their enterprises so that they are able to fulfil their God-given calling — both for the development of their own skills and gifts as well as for the benefit of family and enterprise, state and church."

Sikkel: The trade union "ought to aim both for good labour laws which would ensure the rights of those who work within the enterprise as well as for the direct moral development of the workers."

Talma gave an enthusiastic closing address. He was currently a member of parliament, but he declared that if he became a pastor again he would like to preach for 52 Sundays on "I believe in God Almighty." The next day (January 11, 1905), *Patrimonium* held a special meeting and withdrew the anti-Sikkel resolution of 1903. It appeared that agreement had been reached. Was that indeed the case?

VI

Continuing discussion: Sikkel at the Second Christian Socio-Economic Congress (1909)

The years between 1903 and 1905 were without doubt high points in Sikkel's social activities. In the same year as the conference (1905), he wrote his articles about the wages of labourers in *Hollandia*. These were also published in a booklet. Again he elucidated his vision, now concentrating on wages.

The wage question is not a financial question but a *moral* one. The wages kept back, about which Scripture speaks in the letter of James, are not wages which have been reduced after being agreed upon. No, Sikkel saw it in a much deeper way. "The reduced wage is the wage, earned by one's labour, which violates the moral human fellowship in labour and in God's good gifts." He acknowledged that the wage question was difficult and complicated. Again, he strongly urged the establishment of a labour law that would determine wages. The issue at stake was the "free moral action of the parties concerned." He firmly rejected the notion that those who devote their lives to labour have "no moral right to participate in the discussion of matters that concern their Labour and the human fellowship in the work organization." Again, he explained how he saw the task of the Christian trade unions, now that he had accepted them, namely to call on their fellow labourers "to unite and confer, *under the banner of moral social rights*, of moral fellowship, and of moral action."

Sikkel did not limit the task of the Christian trade union movement to its own circle only: the issue at stake was the moral appeal to the whole world of labour. The whole of Sikkel's social struggle came down to the commandment that the Christian love his neighbour, a commandment which he wanted to see fulfilled concretely in the consultation between employers and employees. The financial issue was never the number one concern with him; it would be solved naturally if the moral appeal to the consciences was heeded. He believed that this moral appeal should originate with Christians, and would then, he was convinced, be heeded by the others.

Indeed, the differences at the conference of 1905 seemed to have been taken away. A sure basis for Christian trade unions had been laid. In 1907, the *Christelijk Nationaal Vakverbond* (Christian National Trade Union Movement) was established and slowly flourished. In the same year, Sikkel became a member of *Patrimonium*'s committee of advice, a position he retained until his death. He remained active during the rest of his life as co-founder and chairman of the sanatorium, *Sonnevanck*, and was appointed to several committees of state. He wrote many articles in *Hollandia* in which he promoted his perspective on the social question and which later were published under the title, *The Social Question*. We do not find new elements in these articles. And yet . . . we get the impression that matters did not develop as he had wished and as he had advocated. Perhaps the time was not yet ripe for it since the primary struggle was to acquire a reasonable social position for the labourer. Only much later would his ideas begin to be implemented. He retained his ideals, and slowly an acknowledgment of his services as a social pioneer grew.

At the Second Christian Social Congress — held in Amsterdam from March 10 through 13, 1919 — in which the socio-economic situation after the First World War was considered, he was not one of the official speakers. But when H. Diemer delivered a paper on "The organization of society," Sikkel did take part in the discussion. Again, his prophetical fervour came to the fore. He called on his fellow congress members to be aware of the injustice in our society: a great deal of the people in our social community, in many ways, lack possessions and rights, and particularly in the field of labour. God gave man on His earth the right to acquire sustenance through labour. That is the solidarity of all of humanity. The "brotherhood of all people in their life on earth is not a revolutionary word, but it is a word from *God*. And we, ministers of the Word, and all Christians have to preach not only the gospel of the forgiveness of sins and eternal life, but also God's word for brotherhood in societal life on this earth and especially in Labour."

The situation that had developed over the years was now such that both classes, the employers and employees, had been organized. The advantage was that negotiations could now be made for wages and conditions. But Sikkel felt that people should not be at peace with that, and so he came back to the old ideals that he still held onto firmly. "But with all that," he continued, "injustice has not been taken away. The armies are now being organized and strengthened for the class struggle, for war between brothers. All sorts of attempts are made to find a way out by means of political power and laws of state, until the inevitable social revolution breaks out." He therefore pleaded again at this second social congress for a democratic organization of enterprise by means of the labour contract, the old ideal of 1903. A constitutional participation in management should be established by the workers within the enterprise, in the communal use of the means of production.

Sikkel received applause at the meeting; the brothers were generous. But had they really understood him? In his reply, Diemer used the opportunity to remind Sikkel that in 1903 he had advocated only a collective judgment by means of the trade unions, which the individual workers could personally join. Indeed, there was a certain evolution in his judgment. This evolution is clearly seen in his last writings.

A respect was growing for Sikkel's services. His son, Rev. D. Sikkel, wrote in a foreword to his father's writings: "my father has often had to wait during his lifetime." That is often the case with pioneers.

In 1920, *Patrimonium* asked him to write a series of articles for their magazine. It is clear that he did so with great enthusiasm. Again he advocated his ideals, now however in closer agreement with the Christian trade union organization; that was also the process of evolution in him. "Not one Christian man may remain outside the trade union," he now wrote. "All Christian trade union chapters should unite in one Christian trade union organization!" He added, however, "With this the last word has not yet been said, but only the *first* word."

Around Pentecost 1920, he made a fiery plea for the international character of the Christian social movement. The law of God's kingdom — one for all and all for one — entailed an international calling. "To seek international ties in the social sphere should not be censured. It is in essence truly social and Christian." Did *Patrimonium* understand his ideals? At its annual general meeting of 1920, he spoke on the subject of "Socialization," but he lamented in his article of May 17, 1920, that even "my Amsterdammers" did not understand him.

He concluded his article of July 24, 1920, with the comment, "until September, the Lord willing!" That did not happen; the Lord had determined otherwise. In August 1920, Sikkel died after a short but serious illness.

VII

Two posthumous writings: about socialization and about the position of the woman

Two of Sikkel's writings appeared after his death. The first, *Socialization*, was his paper delivered to *Patrimonium* in 1920, and the other was on the issue of women, *The Great Future and the Woman*. The latter had become a burning issue after the First World War. Both of these writings show us how much his ideas had developed.

The first paper made a plea for societal input into the productive use of the nation's soils — an old ideal. He also wanted to plead for consumers who ought not to be subjected to the entrepreneur's profit chase. Sikkel rejected the solution of social democracy for society's ills. He felt that social democracy only transforms the state into "Grand-Producer." In that way the worker again becomes a wage slave, although now the slave of a state corporation. The formulation of his objection showed his sharp mind: "The mighty State-Capitalist, supplied with all the power, replaces the much-maligned capitalistic society."

What is striking is that Sikkel is now prepared to grant that the government should be able to intervene, especially where land use is concerned: "The government must encourage the productivity of the national soil, and for the good use of the land let its power be felt." It should intervene to ensure quality products, reasonable price levels, and the best consumption. A council of enterprises should be established to regulate production and consumption. He ended this paper with the words, "Continue with

Christian-social propaganda and action — not least through the goal-directed industry of the Christian social organizations and trade unions — for socialization of production while always honouring the ordinances of God."

In his paper about women, as well, it becomes apparent how much Sikkel's insight had deepened since he spoke at the first Christian social congress. Back then, he had said that it was a thorn in his flesh whenever he saw a woman behind the counter of the post office or telegraph office. Now, however, he points out that not every woman gets married and that therefore each woman needs such education as will make it possible for her to live "with honour" outside of marriage. Women should not be forced to desire marriage "as a form of income or life insurance." The woman must develop her own gifts in society. "No calling or honourable work, in which a woman can and will give herself, is therefore to be denied to the woman as co-worker." He did plead, however, that in her labour the woman would do justice to the phrase "be a helper suitable for him" (Genesis 2). Sikkel did not want this phrase limited to marriage alone but broadened it to the position of women in general — a wide-ranging view indeed.

With regard to the church, too, he regarded the woman's calling in a broader way than many Reformed people then (1920!) and now (1976) do. "The Ministry of the Word, the Eldership, and the Diaconate each need the judgment of the woman and her cooperation, and the Offices in the Church of the Lord are therefore able to demand that judgment and cooperation by having the women vote in God's church." Very sensitively he added, "not because of the social demand of the women, or as an offering on the altar of the spirit of the age, but because 'the Lord has need of it.' " She could, he went on, give helpful service to the diaconate and even, "as a helper suitable" for him, "provide support services in the task of oversight and teaching within the Church of the Lord." She could be asked to lead in prayer. Significantly he added: "here too, the Word of God is broader than is often thought."

VIII

Evaluation

The historian is required not only to draw a picture of his subject but also to evaluate it. He generally does that by considering the judgment of others. Unfortunately that is hardly possible in this case. So far, no one from a Protestant context has given a concise and evaluative study of Sikkel's socio-economic articles and papers. Dr. T. de Ruiter O.F.M., a Roman Catholic, wrote an interesting booklet in 1950, *Ds. J. C. Sikkel en de Organisatie van de Arbeid* (Rev. J. C. Sikkel and the Organization of Labour). Moreover, P. Groen prepared a study for the *Gereformeerd Maatschappelijk Verbond* (Reformed Societal Alliance — a Reformed labour union modeled after Sikkel's ideals) about *Gemeenschap in de arbeid* (Fellowship in labour), in which he dealt critically with Sikkel's organic communal ideas.

We will provide our own evaluation in a number of points:

1. We agree with De Ruiter that Sikkel was dependent on the thinking of Abraham Kuyper. He had been moved by Kuyper's life's work, especially in the social sphere, and tried to develop and make more concrete Kuyper's programme as delivered at the first Christian social congress. Sikkel was one of Kuyper's greatest pupils in the social sector of the Calvinistic revival under Kuyper's leadership.

2. We also agree with De Ruiter's judgment that Sikkel developed the influence which Kuyper had on him into his own

personal views. De Ruiter rightly speaks of this "remarkable man." Without a doubt Sikkel was an original thinker.

3. This originality over against Kuyper becomes evident in his Christ-centred world and life view. For Sikkel, the resurrection of Christ from the dead is pivotal. Thus, Sikkel was little influenced by Kuyper's views on common grace and based his approach to social questions more directly on Scripture, and especially on the Gospel of the crucified and risen Christ.

4. P. Groen's critique of Sikkel's idea of an organic community in the work force is not entirely fair. We also reject the term "organic." Since it is a typically nineteenth century philosophical idea with which we can do very little today, this term does not adequately describe the work community or fellowship. On the other hand, it is not fair to use the Scriptural idea regarding the communion of saints as a critical norm to apply in considering what Sikkel writes about the communion of labour. P. Groen has overlooked the fact that we are dealing with entirely different communions here.

5. The prophetical character of Sikkel's work lies, in the first place, in his Scriptural evaluation of the socialistic ideal of society. He discerned its anti-Christian character, which aimed to make the state all powerful. This criticism remains valid over against the neo-Marxists of today.

6. In the second place, Sikkel's prophetical spirit becomes evident in his struggle for a vision of a society in which the antithesis between capital and labour is taken away through the establishment of enterprise as an organic community. The Christian command-ment to love one's neighbour is Sikkel's driving force here. This love for one's neighbour demands that social warfare be settled

and peace be restored by means of consultation between capital and labour.

7. In the third place, Sikkel's zeal for a Scriptural appreciation of labour as something which belongs to man's task as God's image bearer is of great importance. Labour is not, in the first place, a matter of wages but of fulfilling one's God-given task. The question of wages should be viewed from that perspective.

8. As for criticism of Sikkel, De Ruiter accuses him of "lack of social realism." He adds that Sikkel was ahead of his time. "The socio-economic climate prevailing at that time was not ready for his ideas. Sikkel wanted something like paradise on earth." The latter does not seem correct to us. Sikkel was too convinced of the seriousness of sin to strive for such an ideal. It does seem to us that he overlooked the fact that the time for his ideas had not yet arrived. Because of that he came into violent conflict with the growing Christian trade union movement, which from its side was not sufficiently open to his plea for enterprise fellowship.

9. Even though Sikkel went farther than many in his time in advocating that the government should have power to legislate in the social sphere, he was hampered in this thought by Kuyper's idea of sphere sovereignty. According to Article 36 of the Belgic Confession, the government has the duty to restrain the licentiousness of man. That certainly applies to the socio-economic sphere, as well.

10. When we ask ourselves what we are to do with Sikkel's legacy today, De Ruiter's view is too extreme for us. De Ruiter writes that, "Sikkel's social instinct correctly anticipated the future, including that socio-economic relations would develop toward what today is called the public corporative labour organization."

Sikkel's view of the government's task is too narrow for that. Nevertheless his ideas laid the foundation for such developments. In that respect, many authors from the Christian social movement have rightly appealed to his ideas. On the other hand, the question forces itself on us: Why is it that, despite the social laws and trade organizations now in place in the Netherlands, capital and labour still clash violently so often?

11. To placate the painful social antithesis, we can learn two things from Sikkel. In the first place, Christ's command is fully valid in the social sphere, as well: "You shall love your neighbour as yourself." In the enterprise or the factory we have to deal with our neighbours. The primary concern is with interpersonal relations and they must always be governed by this commandment of Christ. We all have a tremendous task and calling here.

Secondly, we must — in co-operation with others who confess Scripture to be their only guide for socio-economic life — reflect on how and in what way we can make Scriptural ideals reality in the enterprise and factory. We are called to positive action, and then from a few people a great power can emerge. To use Sikkel's words, "We Christians have the calling to proceed, to explore the way, if possible to clear the way, and in love to bring to our fellowmen the witness to the way of God. We Christians must believe that God lives, and that His grace is able to triumph over the spirit of evil (remember Talma's 52 sermons about 'I believe in God Almighty'!). And in faith and with zeal, we must prayerfully look to the victory."

General Index

47

Lectures on Unbelief & Revolution
by Groen Van Prinsterer / Harry Van Dyke

Groen's Masterpiece laid the foundation for Christian Politics in the Netherlands, a foundation on which Abraham Kuyper built. The first half of the book is of an introductory and biographical nature by the translator, Harry Van Dyke.

Subject: Biography / Christian Politics   Age: 16-99
ISBN 0-88906-020-7   Can.$29.95 U.S.$26.95

The Practise of Political Spirituality
by R. Langley McKendree

Episodes from the public career of Abraham Kuyper, 1879-1918
"In an age in which Christians sense a growing warfare with secular humanism, McKendree R. Langley's thorough study of Abraham Kuyper's largely successful application of Christian political ideas to Dutch life is extraordinarily valuable." — Joel Nederhood.

Time: 1879 - 1918   Age: 16-99
ISBN 0-88815-070-9   Can.$9.95 U.S.$8.90

Separation of Church and State
by Norman De Jong & Jack Van der Silk

Since World War II Americans have increasingly come to believe in separation of church and state, yet the majority also want prayer in the public schools and a return to traditional religious values. The authors demonstrate numerous inextricable links which bound church and state together.

Subject: Christian Politics   Age: 14-99
ISBN 0-88815-063-6   Can.$9.95 U.S.$8.90

Christians in Babel by Egbert Schuurman

There was a time when people spoke of a Christian culture. That term is now meaningless. From a biblical point of view our culture can probably be identified as Babylonian. Here man worships various gods as he builds whatever his science and technology enable him to build.

Subject: Church and World   Age: 16-99
ISBN 0-88815-062-8   Can.$4.95 U.S.$3.90